your winner within

your winner within

Always Believe! Holly Hoffman

OWN YOUR POWER, YOUR ATTITUDE AND YOUR LIFE

HOLLY HOFFMAN

Inner Depth, LLC
34328 106th St.
Eureka, SD 57437

Photo Cover: Fadil Berisha Photography New York, NY www.fadilberisha.com
Makeup: Brenda Torre www.brendatorre.com
Hair: Andrew Schmitz, Master Designer

Book cover design, website design and development, marketing by
RockyHayes.com

Book Title Suggestion: Phillip W. Sheppard (The Specialist), Survivor Nicaragua,
Season 22

Website: hollyhoffman.org
Twitter: HollyHoffmanS21

Contents

Acknowledgement

I would like to thank my husband, Charlie, and our children, Austin, Alexandra, and Elizabeth, for their support of me writing this book. You have supported me in ways only family members can – by offering encouragement, instilling confidence when I doubted myself, and loving me through it all.

I would like to thank Elizabeth Hoffman, Corrina Capotrio, Cindy Schumacher, Sally Isburg, Nona Gab and Monica Hilgemann for their help in the editing of this book.

Dedication

I dedicate this book to my mother, Margie Walker, the strongest woman I have ever known. Despite the numerous challenges faced in your lifetime, your personal and emotional strength has never faltered. Words cannot express the gratitude I have for you. You are amazing and I love you!

This book is also dedicated to my brothers, Shaun and Troy Wanner. You were my best friends when we were young and my mentors as I grew into adulthood. You taught me the importance of being an individual, even when it wasn't the cool thing to do, and I am very proud to have you both as my brothers.

My final dedication goes to my husband, Charlie, and our three children, Austin, Alexandra, and Elizabeth. You are the inspiration in everything I do. To my husband, Charlie, who supports me in all endeavors; and to our three children who I am extremely proud of – I love you all!

Remembrance

The Bible says you are to, "Honor thy father and thy mother, and it shall be good unto you." As I was growing up I didn't have much faith in that particular passage, especially when it came to my dad. However, in my maturity I realize his battle with alcoholism and the subsequent impact on our family has shaped me into who I am today. His shortcomings as a father, husband, and overall human being have significantly influenced my own choices and taught me more about life than anyone else. Dad, you will always have a special place in my heart and I love you.

"Nobody can go back and start a new beginning, but anyone can start today and make a new ending."

~Marie Robinson

Foreword

> **"When you have success, there is glory for all. With success and glory come great feelings for one another and recognition of one another's contributions."**

~Coach Jimmy Johnson

I think it fitting to begin this foreword with one of my favorite quotes from the glory days of winning Super Bowl Championships. Winning in the NFL was a major part of who I am and what I strove to achieve for many years – finding winning and unstoppable players to fill every position on my team. Choosing perfect, world-class athletes for my team from an elite group of football players who could each win nearly any major Olympic event was the hardest part of making the right pick.

I met Holly Hoffman in the hardest game I ever played. She always had a winning attitude, was front and center on game day, and never gave up. It almost seemed as if every day was game day for Holly. Holly exemplifies what it takes to persevere in times of extreme fatigue. Through her great work ethic, charisma, and overall positive attitude, she embodies what it means to be a successful person. If there was an NFL draft for a winning attitude, Holly would be my first round draft pick.

Jimmy Johnson, former NFL coach

Holly Hoffman with Jimmy Johnson, the former football coach for the Dallas Cowboys

Preface

Preface

Everyone is faced with challenges in life, but it is our course through those challenges and our reactions toward them that sets us apart as human beings and makes us better individuals. Through the many personal challenges faced in my lifetime, I have realized the importance and power of a positive attitude. We have all heard the common saying – but attitude really is everything. Each of us has a conscious choice to make with regard to attitude – we can have a good one and make the most of our situation in life, or choose to be miserable. Through my own personal challenges, I have recognized the full potential of my inner strength. At times when I felt vulnerable in an unbearable situation I was motivated by the experience and realized I wanted to improve my life by taking more control of it. When you combine a positive attitude with determination, confidence, desire, faith, and perseverance, a certain energy is created that allows your 'winner within' to truly shine.

I was motivated to write this book to inspire you to be the best person you can be and live every day like it is your last. We all struggle in today's world, but it is our reaction to those struggles that shows our character. By having a positive attitude, determination, confidence, desire, faith, and perseverance, you allow yourself to live a more fulfilled life. You are special; you are a winner; and you can become the person you've always wanted to be. You simply need to harness the power within yourself. You can achieve any realistic goal you set – so believe in yourself!

Attitude
Consciously choose your attitude and cast aside outside influence.

Determination
Every accomplishment begins with a decision to try.

Confidence
Belief in yourself is paramount over whether or not others believe in you.

Desire
Stop living your fears and start living your dreams.

Faith
Believe!

Perseverance
Quitting is never an option.

Chapter One
Attitude

"Our attitude toward life determines life's attitude toward us."

~John N. Mitchell

THOUGHTS ON ATTITUDE: I think of attitude as the landscape of your soul. It is your personal view of the world and dictates how you choose to filter what you see and your reactions to the situations you encounter. It encompasses perceptions, emotions, and actions, and may often determine your overall success. One individual may see a patch of beautiful wildflowers growing on a hillside. Another person may see an overgrown patch of native growing weeds – an eyesore and a nuisance.

I have never experienced an epiphany-like moment when I realized the supreme importance of a positive attitude. Rather, it was the honest recollection of my past failures and frustrations and the one thing they had in common – a poor

17

attitude – that made me realize the power and importance of a positive attitude in my daily life.

A positive attitude is not only important when it comes to the major crossroads in life, but in all the small things you do every day. Based on how you perceive a certain situation, you instinctively develop emotions around it. Those emotions are very important, because they often transform into a course of action – either positive which fosters good or negative which perpetuates negativity. By learning to control your emotions, you take control of your reactions and subsequent actions.

While I am a firm believer in the power of a positive attitude, I will admit that attitude alone cannot solve every problem. However, having a positive attitude towards a bad situation will make great strides toward solving life's problems a whole lot easier. Not every situation is going to roll your way; and as much as we hate to face it, some situations are simply beyond our control. The best thing to do is to take a fresh look, a deep breath, and say, "Okay, what can I do to influence the best possible outcome for my situation?" You see, it is ultimately your attitude that shapes your life. If you want to be a successful and fulfilled person, a positive attitude is essential.

The Power of a Simple Smile

"The world is like a mirror - frown at it, and it frowns at you. Smile and it smiles, too."

~Herbert Samuels

Chapter One - Attitude

There is nearly nothing more powerful than a smile. It attracts the attention and subsequent smiles of others and sends happy signals to all who can see it. And, I guarantee you are going to get some smiles back. Think back on a situation when you were having a bad day and someone smiled at you unexpectedly. You smiled back, didn't you? Proof that smiles are contagious, and they attract positive energy. If you continually walk around with a scowl, you are screaming to the world that you have a negative attitude toward life. Consequently, the first impression you make on others, and likely the lasting impression, will be a force field of negativity – driving away opportunities, friendships, and happiness. Walk with your head held high, believe in yourself, and never stop believing there is good in all things if you only open your mind to them.

I'm thinking about the true power of a smile, and I want to share with you the story of a man who helped shape my positive outlook on life. When I became a parent I realized the importance of surrounding myself with optimistic people, and I made a habit of doing so. When you are surrounded by optimism, there is no room left for negativity. One particular man, Gordon Ehmke, made an impact on my life simply because of his positive attitude and his smile.

Gordon and Betty Ehmke

Your Winner Within

When my daughter Alexandra was seven, she sang for an event in our hometown of Eureka, South Dakota, called Appreciation Days. It was a yearly event sponsored by the Eureka Chamber of Commerce as a way of showing their appreciation to people who did their business locally. This popular event was held at the local ballpark and consisted of a meal, paid for by the Eureka Chamber of Commerce, and included a night of music on a typically beautiful summer evening.

I met Gordon by chance, simply because Alexandra performed right after him. He was an amazing singer; but above that, I couldn't help notice his kindness towards others and the fact that he was always smiling. He had a smile that was unforgettable. His kindness, his smile, and his overall optimistic personality left a lasting impression on me.

A couple of weeks later after a trip to our local grocery store, I was loading groceries into the car while trying to contain three young children and get them in the car at the same time. Needless to say, it was a hectic moment and my attitude was definitely sub-par. As if the universe wanted to teach me a lesson in positivity, Gordon came walking around the corner wearing his blue coveralls – and of course, a huge smile on his face. He noticed us immediately and gave Alexandra a compliment on her beautiful voice and performance at the event, and at the same time made my other children feel special as well. With just a friendly demeanor, a few compliments, and a big smile, he changed my attitude and turned an everyday hectic situation into something pleasant.

Later, I discovered that Gordon was the father of my friend, Nona, and he and his wife, Betty vacationed in Eureka each summer. I often saw Gordon around town, and each time he would welcome me with a huge hug and made sure to ask how my day was going. Gordon had a wonderful habit of always putting others first. Over the years, I got to know Gordon better and I consider him an inspiration in my life. His singing was amazing, his personality was unforgettable, and his overall kindness was a gift from God. Gordon would always greet others warmly, and often times with a hug – whether he knew them well or not. His stand-out personality was so contagious that it made people want to be around him. He had a genuinely warm spirit and I looked up to him like a father.

On July 13th, 2011, after living 83 fulfilling years, Gordon passed away peacefully, quietly, and best of all with his dignity. After his passing Gordon's family was flooded with cards and phone calls, but one card the family received was very special. It was from a "well-seasoned" nurse who said, "What an awesome man he was. I have never enjoyed caring for someone as much as I did your dad. He taught me volumes about humility and self-sacrifice. I will be forever touched by his warm, loving heart." The writing in that card was more than just kind words - it was the absolute truth. When I think of Gordon, I cannot help but smile. He touched my life in so many ways because of his amazing attitude toward life. His impact on my outlook on life was huge, and I will forever be grateful.

Next time you are feeling stressed and want to give in to the power of negativity, try to hold a smile on your face (no, a sarcastic smile does not count), and see how it changes your attitude. Just as Gordon Ehmke smiled to comfort those around him, I encourage you to do the same. Put a smile on every day, and I am convinced you will lead a more successful and fulfilled life.

"The only person you are destined to become is the person you decide to be."

~Ralph Waldo Emerson

Exhibit Self-Control

"An attitude of positive expectations is the mark of the superior personality."

~Brian Tracy

If you are able to take control of your attitude, you can control, to a large extent, how others perceive you. As a human being, you are continually being viewed and noticed by others. And, while you may think it is your physical appearance that takes center stage, it is actually your facial expressions and body language that speak volumes. Your attitude directly influences your emotions; and your emotions directly influence how others perceive you. As a very expressive person, I have found it hard to be disciplined with the emotions I display. When I was feeling angry or stressed, the easy route was to wear my heart on my sleeve; and unfortunately, a scowl on my face. Just as yawning is often infectious, so is your attitude. It takes self-control, but I have made a conscious choice in my life not to influence others negatively based on my facial expressions or body language.

Now, there is a deeper level to controlling your emotions and the resulting body language – it is the conscious versus the subconscious. Have you ever been deep in thought at a department store or chatting with friends at a restaurant and saw your reflection unexpectedly in a mirror? Were you surprised at the mildly unfriendly, intent look on your face? On a subconscious level, you may have been doing the math to find the best deal or were just being a really good listener to your friends – but that is not what your body language portrayed. Even though you may have a positive attitude on the inside, you need to consciously translate that to your

23

outside. Always be aware of how you are projecting yourself to the world – you might miss an opportunity or lose out on a great friendship because your body language wasn't inviting. Opposite of that, please also give people a second chance to make a good impression. When I recall some key events that have shaped my life I remember a particular person who intimidated me based on his body language; however, I took the time to get to know him anyway, and my life would be very different had I not given him a second chance.

I started to run track when I was in junior high, and it was during that time I came to know Coach Hermansen. He was a large, intimidating man, regularly seen in athletic shorts with a clip board in his hand and a stop watch around his neck; he was the type of person whose shadow preceded his physical entry into the gymnasium, giving you a split second to decide if you were going to stay for practice (and endure whatever physical torture he had planned for the day to make you a better athlete), or if you would make a mad dash for the door. I must admit, I considered making that mad dash on numerous occasions.

I was faced with a choice. I could stay in track and let this intimidating man, who I was afraid of, morph me into the athlete I desperately wanted to become, or I could quit. It wasn't an easy decision, but I decided that I wasn't going to let the body language and emotions of others dictate my future, and to some degree deprive me of an opportunity. So, I stayed in track. I worked day-in and day-out with Coach Hermansen to improve my skills; and of course, there were days I still wanted to quit, but my decision paid off! As a track runner, I had an undefeated record from my sophomore year through the end of my high school career. I was in the lead position where everybody wanted to conquer the undefeated winner, and it felt really good. You see, Mr. Hermansen is one of those people who, despite his gruff outward demeanor, was a kind, funny, and dedicated man. Throughout the years, he became a father figure to me. I knew I could count on Coach Hermansen to chew me out when I needed it and that he would also be there to encourage me when I fell short of reaching a goal. It scares me to think how my life would be different if I'd chosen to quit that day simply because I was fearful of Coach Hermansen's body language. All those high school friendships forged on the track field – gone; the glory of my undefeated records – gone; the important life lessons of dedication and humility – gone; and most important, my husband, my children, and the life I've loved for the past 30 years – gone! You see, it was Coach Hermansen who introduced me to my husband, Charlie.

As I have demonstrated, body language and attitude are instrumental in how you forge relationships with others. It can be the difference between meeting your future best friend or spending your life wondering why God hasn't allowed your paths to cross. Maybe He has, and your attitude and actions have interfered with His plans.

Remember the Big Picture

"Your attitude will determine how high you can climb in life."

~Anonymous

There are times in life when we all are tested. When every logical path out of the woods resembles an obstacle course – none of which you feel you have the physical or emotional strength to navigate. In those moments when

25

you are faced with challenges you don't want to accept, that is when you learn the most about yourself. Whether it is the realization of fear or the feeling of self doubt, you cannot advance yourself to a higher level until you acknowledge the things you want to change and allow yourself to grow from the experience. Something good can come of any situation if you keep your mind open and your attitude positive. The best way to do this is to step back, take a deep breath, and try to see the big picture. Ask yourself, "Is this something I can control directly?" If it isn't, you can at least control your approach to the solution – and your solution is largely dictated by your attitude.

When you focus on the big picture, you soon realize the importance of not letting the things you cannot control change your attitude. Think about one of those days where everything that could possibly go wrong, did go wrong. Your alarm didn't go off (even though you KNOW you set it). You're now late for work so you jump out of bed, rush through your morning routine, and run to the car. You're pulling out of the driveway when you realize you've forgotten some important documents; you run back inside to grab them only to realize you've locked yourself out of the house. You're wondering how your day could begin any worse. You hit every red light, are stuck in traffic, and your agitation grows as someone cuts you off.

Now stop. Notice your thoughts and emotions. Are they serving you in this situation or contributing to your agitation? Remind yourself how that one car getting in front of you isn't going to make or break the flow of traffic. You are probably going to be late for work and you need to accept that reality. Channel your thoughts toward bettering the situation you are in – call your boss and tell him you will be late. That will alleviate the immediate stress of the situation and allow you to redirect your thoughts toward the positive and focus on the big picture.

When we keep the big picture at the forefront of our minds it shifts our focus from dwelling on the immediate unpleasantness of our situation to thinking about what really matters in our life. One way to shift your focus is to concentrate on things you are thankful for – no matter how small they may be. Whether you are grateful to be in a healthy, loving relationship or just happy there wasn't a line at the coffee shop this morning, take note of what you are thankful for. By acknowledging the good, we crowd out the bad. Armed with good thoughts and the acknowledgement of things you are thankful for, take a step back from your current situation and ask yourself "how does this situation affect the big picture of my life?" If it doesn't, make the best of a bad situation and let the associated negativity fall by the wayside.

However, at times the gravity of a situation may force you to alter your big picture and be a bit selfish by blocking out others for the sake of self preservation. For example, I grew up with an abusive, alcoholic father. As you can imagine, a typical day started out being a bad day and I continually encountered situations that were out of my control. I desperately wanted to discharge the negativity associated with my father, but you see he was part of my big picture. His actions did affect me and weren't something I could easily dismiss as insignificant. So, for a long time I allowed my father's actions to impact my attitude in a negative way. Even though it was my father who was doing the drinking, somehow I felt out of control and embarrassed. It is heartbreaking to turn your back to a loved one, but I knew I had to shift the focus of my big picture so it didn't include him. My dad's choices were his and affected his big picture – not mine. This transition wasn't easy and it surely didn't happen overnight. However, once I realized I could shape my own big picture and choose what was important to me, I felt free.

These experiences and examples are just a handful of many that have allowed me to develop my thoughts on the power of a positive attitude and how important it is to our daily lives. **Smile, exhibit self-control, and always keep your focus on the big picture!**

Remove Negative Influences

While the three components of a positive attitude I've just described may seem fairly easy to implement in your life, beware of the outside factors that come into play. Oftentimes, the biggest obstacle you will encounter on the road to a positive attitude is a negative person. We all know them, those people who have the sole purpose in life to point out why you can't do something, why you won't succeed, and why you shouldn't even try. Our interaction with negative people is inevitable; however, you can influence that interaction in a positive way by controlling your emotions and your actions towards them. For example, if a negative person has said or done something bad towards you, don't think you have to repay them. By repaying evil with evil, you are only stooping to their level and perpetuating negativity. That is not the person you are and certainly not how you want to be perceived. Ironically, sometimes treating negative people with kindness is the best thing you can do. It lifts you out of the gloom and causes the other person to reflect on their own negative actions.

"Your living is determined not so much by what life brings to you as by the attitude you bring to life; not so much by what happens to you as by the way your mind looks at what happens."

~Khalil Gibran

In order to elaborate on this idea, remember when I said that spending time with negative people will be detrimental to your success? It's true! When you surround yourself with people who are of a negative mindset and enjoy spreading their negative influence by putting others down, you are at great risk to assume that same attitude. Just like a positive attitude is contagious, so is a negative one. Surround yourself with positive people to stay positive yourself. If you are not associating with the kind of person you want to be, you need to make a change. If your association with these people is necessary, for whatever reason, you at least need to change the way you think about it.

"You cannot always control circumstances, but you can control your own thoughts."

~Charles Popplestown

You are fully aware of the negative influences in your life, and you need to do something about it. Take action and seize the opportunity to make a positive change. If someone in your family or someone you are spending time with is constantly negative, you need to look them in the eye and encourage them through positive reinforcement. By making upbeat comments back to them, their negative attitude will start to wear off and eventually they will realize "You know, she is right, I need to start focusing on the positive things in my life and stop my bad habit of constantly tearing things apart and thinking negative thoughts." As you work to change their attitude through your own, think about the three things I discussed previously: smiling, exhibiting self-control, and focusing on the big picture. All three things will help you to change a negative person into one who is positive.

Society, as a whole, has generally taught us to look for and focus on the negative in situations and people. Negative people are everywhere; but in reality, every negative person placed on this earth has at least one good quality – you just need to find it. Imagine you are in a room with 50 people and you receive compliments from 49 of them and a negative comment from one. How do you feel and what do you walk out of that room remembering? That one bad thing! You need to focus on the positive in everyone and remember there will always be someone suffering from very low self-confidence who will bring you down in order to feel better about their own shortcomings. That one lone person is likely feeling sorry about their situation and trying to obtain attention through negative comments or actions. So when you encounter negative people, remember there is good in everyone, and you need to help find that good.

> ## "Believe you can and you are half way there."

~Theodore Roosevelt

Keys to Implementation

In this chapter, I've discussed my thoughts on the most important steps to implementing and maintaining a positive attitude and also how to manage the negative influences in your life. However, you may now be asking yourself, "How do I take this information and implement it in my daily life? How do I make it work for me?" It's simple… you can improve your attitude little by little every day by thinking positive thoughts and always working toward improvement. I remember someone telling me "the attitude you bring to a problem will make the difference between failure and success in regard to the problem" – and I firmly believe it. Sometimes stressful situations cannot be avoided. But, by practicing positive thoughts and working toward improving your attitude, a negative situation can always be improved. So, if you are already in a stressful situation and realize you are getting angry, there are a few things you can do to take control and ensure the negative outside factors are not affecting your attitude. Here are some exercises you can do that will put you on a path to improving your attitude:

Exercise One: Breathe, Breathe, And Breathe. First, sit down and take some deep breaths – clearing your mind of all negativity and thinking positive thoughts. It is surprising how deep, conscious breathing can open your mind and put a positive picture in your mind. I often visualize myself on a beach or enjoying a vacation with my family. Since you cannot control every situation or how others treat you and what they say to you, your best line of defense is controlling your emotions, one deep breath at a time.

Exercise Two: Train Your Brain. You've heard the term "practice makes perfect," right? Well, it isn't only true in sports. The more effort you put into training your brain to react positively, the better it will perform. Start a routine every evening before you go to bed – sit at the end of your bed and say a prayer. Prayer works and prayer helps. After you've prayed, it is likely the next thing you will remember is your alarm clock buzzing, waking you abruptly into a new day. First, acknowledge the buzzing and turn it off! Then, pay attention to the first thing that pops in your brain. If it is anything negative, sweep it out of the way in exchange for something optimistic. Studies have found that negative thinking can actually hurt your health and, in my experience, ruin a perfectly good day. It is immensely important to get up and think about something positive. Start that day off right!

"Choosing to be positive and having a grateful attitude is going to determine how you're going to live your life."

~Joel Osteen

Now that you are out of bed, rested and in good spirits, think about your priorities for the day and make your "to-do" list. Let's face it, life is stressful more often than it is not, and there is always a never ending list of things to do. Don't be overwhelmed. Focus on the things that you can realistically accomplish in a day and start whittling away at your list. Personally, I recommend putting the most stressful, nagging things at the top of the list. I feel more refreshed in the morning and ready to tackle anything. Plus, when I get something out of my head and down on paper it tends to stop bouncing around my consciousness, distracting me for the rest of the day. The task is there in black and white, it is the first thing on my list, and I can't move through my day until that first ugly chore is DONE. There is something special that happens when you physically write something down. Your conscious and subconscious minds become one, and it lessens the anxiety of a task. What previously was in your subconscious and filled with emotion and worry is now a simple statement on a piece of paper. Sometimes you have to distance yourself or de-personalize a task in order to complete it.

Exercise Three: Self-Reflection: Although it may take you some time to become comfortable with this technique, self-reflection can be a great attitude booster. Every day, take some time to write down your thoughts. The key here is these need to be your honest thoughts and not ones you write in case someone finds your secret self-reflection notebook. The sole purpose is to help you, and you can't do that if you aren't honest with yourself. Also, don't be afraid to share your thoughts with other people, especially if they are in a position to encourage you. Other people can't encourage and energize you if they don't know what goal you are working toward. Don't be afraid to ask your friends and loved ones to support your beliefs. If they have your best interest in mind, they will be happy to throw some cheerful words of encouragement your way.

Exercise Four: Create a Code to Live By. This is going to be slightly different for each of you, but take some time to craft a few statements you truly believe in and that you truly believe will influence your positive attitude and emotions. Write them down; carry them with you. As you make your way through the day, if you start feeling a little run down, refer to your code and rely on it for strength and guidance. It will only remind you of what is important to you. Here are a few of the mental habits I choose to uphold as part of my code:

- Do not live in the past

- Do not try to change the inevitable

- Never let the way people treat you, affect you

- Avoid negativity and keep a positive attitude

Exercise Five: Acknowledge Your Emotions. Generally, I feel that emotions have an unwarranted, bad reputation. From the time we are young, we are taught to suppress our emotions out of courtesy to others and for the sake of guarding them. There is a very fine line here between suppressing your emotions and acknowledging them. Suppress, no; acknowledge, yes! In order to develop a positive attitude, you need to be able to acknowledge your emotions on a conscious level, reflect on why you feel the way you do, and develop a positive plan of action to address them. You can't control something you won't acknowledge. For example, if you are in a verbal confrontation, your immediate response is likely to yell or insult your adversary. Take a moment to recognize your anger and find the root cause. Sometimes, the

"It's not who you are that holds you back from doing something, it's who you think you are not."

~Attributed to Hanoch McCarty

best reaction to a bad situation is no reaction at all. If you can acknowledge your emotions and control them, you will take great strides to creating the beautiful life you envision. Conversely, if you suppress your emotions, you run the risk of reaching full emotional capacity which can lead to a blow up or meltdown.

In conclusion, I want to remind you to smile, exhibit control over your emotions, and keep the big picture firmly planted in your mind. You do not need to deal with every problem in your life at the same time – or at this very moment. Take one step at a time, keep your attitude positive, and deal with every situation in a productive manner. Understand you will make mistakes – it happens! Pick yourself up (giggle at yourself if you need to), learn from your mistakes, and keep moving forward. The ability to brush it off and keep a positive focus will make you the strong, positive person you want to become. Your attitude is everything!

"Change your thoughts and you change the world."

~Norman Vincent Peale

"If you make the unconditional commitment to reach your most important goal, if the strength of your decision is sufficient, you will find the way and the power to achieve your goal."

~Robert Conlin

Chapter Two
Determination

"Every accomplishment starts with the decision to try."

~Unknown

THOUGHTS ON DETERMINATION: Determination is focusing every cell of your being toward an end result. You've decided to pursue something that is worth accomplishing and you drive towards it. *No whining, no looking back, and no quitting!*

Determination is the cornerstone of self-improvement and ultimately, success. Without it, neither would be possible. In today's busy world, there is no lack of suggestion on what we should be determined to do next – from running a marathon for charity to leading your local neighborhood watch. My message to you is this: always be completely determined towards a goal; however, be selfish and selective about where you choose to focus your energy. Focus on what is important to you and don't let others obligate your time without your permission. For example, if you make a commitment to run that marathon for charity, you have to do it on your own terms. You need to set aside time to train, make sure you have the proper running gear, and most important, take that first step of the run. You must be determined and self-motivated to accomplish your goals – it is vital to your success.

Why is determination vital to success? Because when you are determined, you hold yourself accountable for your actions; and people who make themselves accountable are typically more successful than those who do not. I believe we each have an innate sense of determination to finish what we start, if only from a perspective of pure curiosity to find out if we can achieve a goal. The fact is, you may have raw talent at something, but without executing that innate determination, you may never become aware of it. Determination and persistence are more relevant to success than talent, because without them talent is wasted.

Success means different things to different people, but the common factor we all share is that we must have determination in order to achieve and maintain success. Successful people use their innate determination to achieve extraordinary results in their everyday life. I believe there are three major, interwoven components that comprise extraordinary determination: willfulness, discipline, and ambition. Willfulness and discipline will allow you to achieve a goal; however, you must first have the ambition to realize the full benefit of the other components. When you surround yourself with ambitious people, like a plant that has been given the perfect amount of water and sun, you give yourself the best possible environment to achieve your goal. Here is where the self-perpetuating cycle of ambition and success reaches its full capacity – when you are ambitious, you achieve your goals: when you achieve your goals, your ambition is increased. Simply put, through determination and ambition you will set yourself on a successful path to achieve your goals, subsequently making you a more confident person who wants to set and achieve even more goals.

Throughout my life, I have instilled within myself a deep appreciate for determination. Growing up in a household with an alcoholic father caused my family, and especially my mom, to struggle financially and emotionally. I remember my mom working three jobs on a regular basis; and during the summer months, I also worked three jobs in order for us to make ends meet. I did this because I was determined to lessen my mom's burden and to ensure we had the bare essentials to get by. I have learned a lot about myself through those childhood experiences and over the years have channeled those hardships towards good in the form of motivation, determination, and being the best parent I can be to my own children. By doing so, I was able to maintain my role as disciplinarian during my children's teenage years. I strove to be a good parent and not a best friend to my children. I realized early on the importance of providing structure in our household and teaching our children to develop their own determination. At times this was difficult, but I realized it was critical to their success as individuals. I was able to do this by using the determination and motivation instilled within my character at a young age. Additionally, this approach allowed my husband and me to ensure our children had the tools to become the best they could possibly be. I am involved in all of my children's lives, and I enjoy celebrating their accomplishments. We are truly blessed with three wonderful children and the hard work we have invested in them has definitely paid off.

"The difference between the impossible and the possible lies in a person's determination."

~Tommy Lasorda

Childhood aside, there have been many other experiences throughout my life which have allowed me to foster my innate sense of determination and become the person that I am today. One of those very experiences occurred in the summer of 2008 when our daughter, Alexandra, was crowned Miss South Dakota.

Alexandra Hoffman Miss South Dakota 2008
Photo by Evans Gallery Sioux Falls, SD

The evening of Alexandra's crowning was an exciting one filled with many memories and endless photos. It wasn't until after the pageant that I looked at photos of myself taken that night, and I realized I had turned into someone I did not like. It was obvious from the photos I was not taking care of myself like I should, and I basically let myself go.

I was overweight; I was unhappy; I was tired all the time; and I had very low self-esteem. I knew I hadn't been feeling like myself, but it wasn't until I looked at the photos from the pageant that I realized I needed to make a positive change in my life. Looking back, I had turned into one of the biggest junk food junkies ever, no exaggeration. I was spending a lot of time in the car which meant endless stops at convenient stores where I would pick up any junk food that caught my eye instead of eating healthy. I was using my time on the road as an excuse for my bad eating habits and inability to exercise. It was difficult, but I forced myself to acknowledge I was using excuses – I had to stop relying on them and just fix the problem. My biggest excuse, which is a common one, was, "I don't have the time." I needed to realize that if I wanted results badly enough, and if I was determined enough, I would make the time to implement a positive change in my life.

After realizing that I could find the time, I worked toward improving my self-image and regaining my self-confidence. My first step was realizing I needed to make a lifestyle change and stay committed to that change. I started by creating an exercise program for myself. I began slowly, investing 30 minutes every day. I started by walking and that soon progressed into jogging. With every step I felt my innate determination growing inside me again. By the time I reached my goal, I was running three to five miles, five times a week, and it felt so wonderful!

I took the initial step for myself based on my ambition and determination for change, but encouragement from friends was very important. If you need some help finding your self-determination, it is a great idea to utilize your friends as motivators. When I started exercising, I walked with my close friend and neighbor, Cindy Schumacher. We encouraged each other to reach our goals and held each other accountable. On days where I didn't want to find the time to exercise, I thought about how Cindy and I were accountable to each other, and that was motivation for me to show up every time. Involving friends in my journey was a tremendous help toward achieving my goals.

Throughout the first phase of trying to accomplish my goals with sheer determination, I realized how important it was to start slowly in order to achieve my goal. If I had tried to run five miles on the treadmill that very first day, I likely wouldn't have succeeded. And, not only would I not have succeeded, I would have been discouraged from trying again the next day. Don't put yourself in a position to be discouraged and lessen your determination. Was I ever discouraged in my journey? Yes! I wanted to quit many times, and I had second thoughts even more often. However, I never let those feelings get in the way of my success. I never let those feelings reverse my new-found determination. Even when I was setting the alarm at bedtime for my 5:30 a.m. workout, I would tell myself, "Be prepared, because you will get up." Hitting the snooze button was not an option.

Even though I was now determined and making progress toward my goal, the fact remained that I was still traveling a lot. While I couldn't control how much travel was required in my busy life, I could control the impact that travel had on my life. As a healthy countermeasure, I routinely carried my workout clothes in the car and made a point to find the workout room or swimming pool in the hotel where I was staying. By setting aside time to work out, it became a part of my daily routine, and it became a part of my life. I had to stay committed, and I had to have the determination to keep going.

Another vital component to achieving my goal was eating healthy, and I clearly needed to make some changes. Instead of relying on convenience stores and gas stations for my lunch or afternoon snack, I started carrying a cooler filled with yogurt, fruits, veggies, and water. I always had something at my fingertips, and it was always something healthy. I soon realized that what I put into my body greatly affected what I got out of it. It didn't take long before I started feeling better about myself, more confident, and most important, like myself again. Based on my success, I gained more determination and began to make a list of monthly goals I wanted to accomplish. Whether it was to lose another pound or add an extra half mile on the treadmill, I learned that I had to push myself, because my success would be determined by my determination. Yes, there were mornings where I did not want to get out of bed, but I forced myself. I made the decision to be successful and was determined to achieve my goal.

Once I started seeing results, I realized there was no turning back – I had to keep going. I was more motivated than I had ever been to achieve my goal. Within 19 months, I was able to lose 40 pounds! It was all about staying committed and determined. When you feel good about yourself, it is amazing how your life changes. I went from being self-conscious and unhappy with myself to becoming energetic and more self-confident. Now, I must be honest and admit my journey was not traveled on a road of pure success and yours probably won't be either – we're human! There will be times when you think you are failing and you want to give up; but if you push those thoughts aside, continue to believe in yourself, and tell yourself you can do it – you will! It is in the realization of your failures and commitment to make a change that you will be able to push aside the negative thoughts in your mind and stay on course toward achieving your goal. Stay committed; embrace your innate determination; become the person you want to be.

"Your chances of success in any undertaking can always be measured by your belief in yourself."

~Robert Coolier

"Nobody who ever gave their best regretted it."

~George Halas

Keys to Implementation

In this chapter, I've discussed my thoughts on determination, ambition, and the importance of being self-motivated. Now, it is your turn to reflect on yourself and give some thought to how you intend to implement these values into your daily life – how to make it work for you! Determination, ambition, and self-motivation mean different things to different people, which is why it is so important to create a customized plan. Here are some exercises to get you started:

Exercise One: Visualize. The first step to visualizing the new you is acknowledging there is something out of balance in your life. Then, you must reach deep inside yourself to determine what you are willing to do to restore that balance. The first step toward change is to visualize yourself in your new role – whether it is a thinner, more healthy version of yourself, or crossing the finish line at the end of that marathon. Close your eyes – visualize yourself. Now, as you're visualizing yourself in this new role and you're smiling at yourself from your mind's eye, create a very specific goal you want to achieve. The more specific you can be the better, but make sure your goal is attainable. You don't want to shoot too high or too low; you want to push your boundaries without setting yourself up for failure. Being realistic is vital to success.

Exercise Two: Create a Plan. After you've decided upon your realistic and attainable goal, write down the steps you need to take on a daily basis to achieve it. Once your goal is defined and you understand the steps you must take to achieve it, it is time for that self-determination and motivation to kick in. Motivation is that pinch that gets you started, but you have to push yourself every single day to create healthy habits that align with your goal. Will there be days of discouragement? Absolutely, but you need to summon your inner strength and motivation to stay the course. Inner strength is the key to achieving your goals; and when you learn to really apply yourself, things tend to fall into place and achieving your goal will soon become easier. However, you need to apply yourself daily. This includes being organized and self-motivated. A determined person will take the first step into a seemingly impossible maze of obstacles and find a way to succeed, while an undetermined person will stumble and fail at that very first step – or never step into the maze at all. All it takes is that first step, so take it! It is from that initial step, the subsequent results, and your continued motivation that you will be successful.

Exercise Three: Keep Your Motivation Fresh. There are simple things you can do every single day to ensure you keep your determination alive. I feel that mornings are very important and a great opportunity to spend just a few minutes of alone time with yourself to say, "Today is going to be a great day and I am going to seize the opportunities I am presented with." By channeling good thoughts and starting the day with a positive attitude, you also channel your inner determination. Try to stay organized throughout your day, but don't sweat the small stuff. If you are a mom, you may greet the day knowing that your kids need to get ready for school, you have to get to your job, and there is endless housework waiting for you. Does it really matter that you have a little dust behind your knick-knacks or the remnants of breakfast are still visible on your dining table? No, it really does not matter. Focus your motivation and determination toward what really needs doing and what is critical to your success. Remember that family is the most important thing, so take time for your children and your spouse. Help them get their days started with a positive attitude by offering love, support, and keeping your positive attitude visible. Of course, you must also focus an adequate amount of time on yourself. If you feel discouraged throughout the day, try to stay determined to accomplish the tasks at hand, talking yourself through difficult times. Tell yourself you believe in yourself and the goals you are working toward. Motivation and encouragement from other people goes a long way; however, you need to have the strength to believe in yourself, even if no one else does, to find your innate determination. Focused determination in your everyday life will accomplish great things.

"The difference between the impossible and the possible lies in a person's determination."

~ Tommy Lasorda

Chapter Three
Confidence

"With confidence, you can reach truly amazing heights; without confidence, even the simplest accomplishments are beyond your grasp."

~Author Unknown

THOUGHTS ON CONFIDENCE: The essence of confidence is belief in your ability to accomplish anything you are determined to do. This is an understanding within yourself that you can tackle the challenges life throws at you, and for the most part, you will be successful. You may not always succeed on the first attempt, but you believe in yourself enough to keep trying until you do.

Self-confident people demonstrate power and grace which is noticed the instant they walk into a room. They have a bold stride, they hold their head high, and they look you in the eye when they talk to you. Their belief in themselves is apparent as they are not afraid to take on challenges or fail. Oftentimes, confidence stems from first-hand knowledge of a task. If you are aware of your strengths and weaknesses, it will be easier to navigate difficult situations, because you can quickly rely on your strengths for guidance. By understanding your strengths you have the ability to exude confidence in any situation, even ones you haven't encountered previously. Overall, confident people:

- Have the ability to function in nearly any situation

- Believe in their ability to accomplish tasks others might find difficult or impossible

- Have the ability to lead and take charge

- Believe they can do things well

- Are not afraid of failure

Having said that, I don't believe the majority of us were born with an innate sense of self-confidence. Our confidence is shaped as we learn and grow and navigate our way through life. It is influenced by good parenting, socialization with others, and even external factors. However, the most important influence on our self-confidence is the process of accepting challenges, finding our own solutions, and succeeding.

One experience that shaped my self-confidence occurred when I was a sophomore in high school. I received an invitation to compete for the Miss South Dakota Teen USA title. At first I was very hesitant; after all, I didn't know anything about beauty pageants and considered myself more of an athlete than a beauty contestant. Still, the opportunity intrigued me. I confided in my mom, and we agreed it would be a good opportunity for me to strengthen other aspects of character – what could it hurt to try?

In order to participate, I needed some material things like an evening gown and a stage costume; but if I was really going after this, I needed some serious work on my stage presence and self-confidence. I started small by looking at pictures in magazines and visualizing myself on stage, thinking about what I'd be wearing, my hair and makeup, and my posture. However, the closer it came to pageant day the more I realized I was not as prepared as I needed to be. When the big day finally arrived I was very nervous, but something deep inside kept urging me to be confident. Throughout the pageant, I made a conscious effort to channel my self-confidence and do my best. I remember the beginning of the pageant very clearly. I approached the microphone to introduce myself; I stood confident and proud and announced the county I represented. I may not have had the best gown, the best stage costume, the best makeup, or even the greatest hairstyle, but I had confidence in myself. I did not end up winning the Miss South Dakota Teen USA title that year, but I was proud of my performance and the self-confidence I gained through the experience.

Another aspect of my life which has made me realize the importance of self-confidence is my marriage. Charlie and I were married at a young age, and through the years, I've learned we both need to believe in ourselves before we can believe in each other. I fully appreciate his continual support; but in order to maintain my own self-confidence, I need to challenge myself and have my own successes in life. Charlie is always there for me; however, it is through the act of succeeding on my own that I am able to gain self-confidence.

"Confidence comes from not always being right but from not fearing to be wrong."

~Peter McIntyre

Chapter Three - Confidence

The journey of parenting is another great example in which I realized the importance of self-confidence. When our children were young, I recognized they were very talented swimmers. As a parent, I wanted to give them every opportunity to develop their talent, so I started a swim team. You are probably thinking I must have had some knowledge or background in the sport myself to take on such a large undertaking – wrong! I knew nothing of the sport and much less about coaching it. Even so, I embraced the challenge and put one foot in front of the other toward my goal. I spent countless hours on the phone talking to other coaches, watching videos, and reading a lot of books. The creation of the team meant I had to be confident in myself as well as confident in other people. In the beginning, there were times when I didn't know exactly what I was doing. However, I kept learning and growing, and ultimately was successful. In addition to developing many state champions, our team won several awards throughout the state and I was awarded "Coach of the Year" a few times. Even though we were a small team, we were known throughout the State of South Dakota and surrounding states as the team to beat. It was my motivation and determination that got the ball rolling, but it was my self-confidence that made me and the team successful.

As a coach, one of my goals was to teach my swimmers and their parents to be confident. I knew from my own experience as an athlete that they would not be successful if they weren't confident in their ability. It took some hard work, but I like to think each member of my swim team learned a thing or two about confidence – and hopefully applied it to other areas of their lives. From a personal perspective, this goal of instilling self-confidence in all my swimmers really paid off. Two of the members of the team were my daughters, Alexandra and Elizabeth, and they both became successful collegiate swimmers. Alexandra swam for the South Dakota State University Jackrabbits and Elizabeth for the University of South Dakota Coyotes. Both broke many records during their collegiate careers and embody my message of self-confidence.

In addition to being successful swimmers, both of our daughters also competed in pageantry. Alexandra was crowned Miss South Dakota Teen USA 2006 and Miss South Dakota 2008; Elizabeth was crowned Miss South Dakota Teen USA 2008. Preparing to compete in the state pageants was a significant commitment, but preparing for the national pageants took even more time and dedication. As part of the girls' preparation, they learned to believe in who they were and to always be confident. I would remind them to be poised on stage and to always be aware of their body language. Positive body language is important in all aspects of life; but in pageantry, it is vital. When you're on a stage, self-confidence can be judged in an instant, and you can't get that instant back if you weren't prepared.

Alexandra Hoffman (left) swam for South Dakota State University and Elizabeth (right) swam for the University of South Dakota

Elizabeth Hoffman graduate of the University of South Dakota - Photo by Jolosch Photography

I'm proud to say both of our daughters gained confidence through pageantry, and the life lessons learned through their experience has paid dividends in other areas of their lives. When Elizabeth was a senior in high school she was faced with the decision of where to continue her education. With so many choices, the decision was a difficult one; but with dreams of becoming a physician, she needed a university that would best prepare her for medical school. Elizabeth decided to apply to the University of South Dakota and, when doing so became aware of an Alumni Students Scholar Program. This program would allow her to be pre-accepted into medical school as a freshman in college. She filled out the application and was thrilled to hear she had been selected to move on to the interview process – at least until the full realization set in that she would interview in front of a panel of nine doctors. I wasn't allowed in the interview room with Elizabeth that day, but I remember telling her to show self-confidence from the moment she walked in the room, display conscious, positive body language, and answer the questions with confidence. When you have self-confidence anything is possible.

Based on the self-confidence Elizabeth developed through her life experiences over a span of seventeen short years, she was able to impress the interview panel with poise, confidence, and of course, intelligence. As she was leaving the room, one of the doctors pulled her aside and said, "Elizabeth, please tell your parents they have done a wonderful job." Four incoming freshmen were awarded the scholarship that year, and Elizabeth was one of them.

Conquering Low Self-Esteem

Undoubtedly, self-confidence is important in every aspect of life. However, it is unrealistic to believe that a person can maintain their self-confidence in every situation, all the time. Sadly, self-confidence is a lot like trust in the fact that it takes years to develop and can be destroyed in an instant. For most of us, low self-esteem (or the lack of self-confidence) happens slowly over time through the regular grind of our daily lives. Our self-confidence wears down a little bit every time we make a mistake, fail, feel guilty, neglect ourselves, or encounter a myriad of other things. In these situations, when life has worn you down and you feel self-doubt, you must pick yourself up and move forward. After all, failure is not falling down; failure is staying down.

When trying to overcome a lack of self-confidence it is important to identify where your self-doubt is coming from. To get yourself thinking on the topic, ask yourself these questions:

- Do I believe in myself?

- Do I love myself?

- Am I out of my comfort zone?

- Do I have feelings of guilt, anxiety, or panic?

- Am I able to say "no" to others?

- Am I happy with the way I am living my life?

If you are willing to reflect on the honest answers to these questions, you will be on track to regaining your self-confidence. Working through the obstacles that stand between you and your confidence can change your entire outlook and allow you to enjoy life more. Confident people are not afraid to be themselves, whereas non-confident people try very hard to be someone they are not. You have absolute control over your own confidence, and it is imperative you focus on the present and forgive yourself for any shortcomings you have had in the past. If you do this, you can regain your confidence at any point in your life, regardless of past experiences. If you settle for what you are dealt in life, whether it is due to a lack of self-confidence or some other factor, you will never experience an incredibly rewarding life filled with confidence, passion, and enthusiasm. There is no shame in wanting more self-confidence, just as there is no shame in wanting more out of your life. Accept every situation you are faced with and, as you learned in Chapter One, have a positive attitude. The power of a positive attitude can change your world.

"The greatest barrier to success is the fear of failure."

~Sven Goran Eriksson

Keys to Implementation

In this chapter we've established the importance of developing self-confidence and maintaining it throughout your life in order to live your best life. Now, let's talk about why self-confidence is absolutely critical to your success. Self-confident people inspire confidence in others, including peers, coworkers, customers, and friends. It is this synergy of confidence and belief in one another that leads to great things. You've heard how people get stuck in vicious cycles, right? Well, there is a cycle that is the opposite – the cycle of success! It's simple really – confident people are successful; when you enjoy success, you have a positive attitude toward life. After a while, these three elements start to feed into one another and you become unstoppable in what you can achieve. That is the cycle of success!

We all must take personal responsibility for our lives and our careers by developing self-confidence to improve our overall sense of self. Here are some tips to building your self-esteem:

Exercise One: Surround Yourself With Positive People. Just as a smile is contagious, so is positivity. When you surround yourself with confident people who are in control of their lives and their careers, you will be motivated to exhibit those qualities in your own life. Seek out positive and encouraging people who will care about you and your goals. By surrounding yourself with positivity and confidence, you will realize the cycle of success I talked about earlier and all the happiness that goes with it. Ultimately, you must have confidence in order to nurture your own success, and being around people who have mastered that is extremely beneficial.

Exercise Two: Develop Your Own Sense of Self-Confidence. Consistent self-confidence building is imperative to long lasting self-confidence. It is something you need to work at every day to counteract all those insignificant blows to it during your daily life. The keys to developing your own sense of self-confidence is the essence of this chapter, but remember to start with a positive attitude, an honest assessment of your strengths, and the motivation to change. As humans, we are blessed with the ability to free ourselves from self-doubt and by doing so, we can continually regain our self-confidence. Building self-esteem must be something you do for yourself, not anyone else. It is never too late to become confident and live the life you always dreamed of. In order to master self-confidence, you must have faith in yourself and your ability to handle any situation presented to you.

Exercise Three: Utilize Positive Self-Talk. Let's face it. There is no better person to deliver a pep talk on what's been bothering you than yourself. By utilizing self-talk, you can remind yourself of the strengths you have developed, the things you do really well, and offer encouragement on your shortcomings. This technique may be a little uncomfortable at first, but it will have a huge impact on your optimism and self-confidence. The more optimistic you are, the more confidence you will have and the more successful you will be.

In addition to the exercises I just talked about, here are some suggestions to instantly build your self-confidence:

Dress for Success. Although clothes certainly do not make the person, they will affect the way you feel about yourself. Take pride in your appearance! When you know you don't look good, your body language screams it to the rest of the world. You are less likely to interact with others and more likely to miss an opportunity in your path. I'm not saying you need to buy a new wardrobe and spend a lot of money, but make sure you have a few "go to" outfits that make you feel confident and successful.

Let Your Confidence Shine. Do you remember your mother telling you to sit up straight and smile? I sure do, and I think she was on to something big. Two of the best ways to judge someone's self-confidence is by the way they carry themselves and the smile (or lack thereof) they have on their face. People who walk confidently always seem to know where they are going and how to get there. Make a habit of using good posture and keep your head held high when you walk into a room. Stand up and be proud of who you are!

Praise and Encourage Yourself. Many people associate self-confidence with arrogance, and at the risk of seeming arrogant, do not exhibit their self-confidence outwardly. It is perfectly fine to pat yourself on the back, encourage yourself through self-talk, and visualize yourself succeeding. As Henry Ford said, "Whether you think you can or think you cannot, you are right." You are your worst enemy, so rid yourself of negative self-talk and replace it with positive.

However, as you work to develop your self-confidence, it is important to understand the difference between confidence and just plain arrogance. Confidence is acknowledging your achievements and having pride in your successes. It is not purposely touting your accomplishments in the faces of others in order to gain their respect or recognition – because you won't. It is perfectly fine to give yourself a pat on the back, but it is never acceptable to be overly boastful of your success. Confidence does not seek out approval. If you are truly confident, you will not need the constant praise of others to feel happiness – you will already know it yourself. Arrogant people often need self-satisfaction from others and they tend to put people down in order to make themselves look better. Confidence is a useful tool for everyday life, but arrogance will quickly set you on a path leading the opposite direction from the goals you want to achieve.

Chapter Three - Confidence

"Success comes in cans, not cannots."

~Author Unknown

I would like to close this chapter by reminding you that the confidence you have in yourself will inspire others. Confident people are contagious. They radiate positive energy and have the mindset of being unstoppable versus afraid when it comes to accepting challenges and living life. Throughout your journey of achieving self-confidence, you will realize the importance of building self-confidence from within and limiting the influence of external factors. Just as you must be confident in yourself before you can be confident in others – don't expect others to believe in you before you do.

You must have complete self-confidence to be successful, but that does not guarantee you will be successful in every challenge you accept. Don't let that discourage you or drain your self-confidence. Keep a positive attitude, remind yourself of the motivation and determination behind your goals, and keep trying! Never feel you shouldn't have attempted a goal based on the fact that you didn't succeed. A self-confident person will learn from the situation and use those tools to succeed in the next attempt. Once your confidence is developed and you are able to maintain it on a daily basis, you have the tools to conquer any situation you encounter. You will believe in yourself, trust your actions and judgment, and even laugh at yourself.

"Our destiny changes with our thought; we shall become what we wish to become, do what we wish to do, when our habitual thought corresponds with our desire."

~Orison Swett Marden

Chapter Four

Desire

"In order to succeed, your desire for success should be greater than your fear of failure."

~Bill Cosby

THOUGHTS ON DESIRE: Desire transcends beyond a basic need or simple want; it is connected to your being on an instinctual level. It is a deep longing for something that is missing in your life, whether it is for a particular state of mind, the accomplishment of a dream, or for the goodwill of another person.

Take a moment to think about what you desire. Perhaps it is to be a good parent, to own your own business, or even to be a successful politician or musician. A desire will often surface in your mind as a reoccurring thought or daydream. It may not always be at the forefront of your mind; but when your mind wanders, it typically leads back to your desires. It is these things you truly desire that you should set your goals around because desire is an innate motivator. If you couple desire with a positive attitude, determination, and confidence, you are well on your way to achieving your goals.

In order to understand the magnitude of desire, imagine yourself in a situation with someone who has made it clear they do not want to be there. We've all experienced it - picture the husband seated outside the women's dressing room at the mall or the wife seated on a frozen lake ice fishing in sub-zero temperatures – not happy campers! The obvious solution here is to surround yourself with positive people who want to engage in life, even if it is a little out of their comfort zone. However, that is not always within our control. The fact is, when someone is so intent on disengaging from a situation or an event, their bad attitude spreads like a virus and they actually take energy away from it. You can be in a room of 25 people and the force field of negativity coming from that one person can reverse the mood of the entire group. Now, imagine the opposite. You are at an event where every individual is happy to be there and truly enjoying their interaction with others. Their desire to be there creates an environment of collaboration and positivity where people can share their thoughts, ideas, goals, and desires.

Life is comprised of situations and events; and in order to live a fulfilled life you need to engage in the situations that correspond to your desires. Be where you want to be; but if you can't, at least approach the situation with a positive attitude so you don't remove energy from a situation someone else desires. When you search for, identify, and choose to live with desire, your overall sense of fulfillment in life increases. By acknowledging your innate desire and allowing it in your life, you will feel energetic, creative, courageous, vibrant, and connected to the goals you wish to achieve. The best thing about living a life filled with desire is it fosters joy and fulfillment.

"Desire is the starting point of all achievements, not a hope, not a wish, but a keen pulsating desire which transcends everything."

~Napoleon Hill

The process of seeking out your desires is highly intuitive. You must have the courage to go where you are drawn and trust your instincts have led you in the right direction. Once you realize your desire it is natural to feel energetic and excited, but you may also feel fear. Sadly, many of us are not living our dreams because we are too busy living our fears. For example, I have always had a fear of flying. My pulse would race and my body began to shake at the first boarding call. Often times I could alleviate my fear somewhat by having family and friends fly with me, but I knew that I couldn't always rely on others to quell my fear. I had to do it myself. A couple years ago I had to fly to Los Angeles – alone – and I almost missed a great opportunity because I was held back by fear. Instead of letting my fear ruin the opportunity, I channeled my desire rid myself of this fear into positive energy. It wasn't easy, but I put my fear aside and got on that airplane. In retrospect, being in this situation taught me never to let fear or doubt control my desire. The one seemingly small act of getting on an airplane alone greatly influenced my desire to work toward independence. When you push forward without fear, it's amazing how quickly a challenge turns into an opportunity. By conquering your own fears, you allow yourself to see a new perspective on life and achieve the dreams you didn't know you even had. You will be successful in life, but only if you have the desire to do so. Now, I can't wait to board a plane for a new adventure.

Keys to Implementation

So, how do you set your desire in motion? How do you learn to acknowledge your instinctual desire and channel that motivation to pertinent situations in everyday life? Here are some tools to help you:

Exercise One: "I Can." In order to foster and maintain desire in your life, you must include two very important words in your vocabulary – "I can." If you adapt your lifestyle around the mantra of "I can", versus "I cannot" – you will be well on your way to success. Strive toward making desire a part of your daily life and implement the "I can" approach into your self-talk exercises. These two simple words have the power to influence a positive attitude, motivate, and encourage – all key indicators of success.

Exercise Two: Channel Your Desire. We've talked a lot about desire and the importance of it in your life. However, it is imperative you understand that desire should only be expressed and utilized in appropriate situations. True desires are developed on an instinctual level based on the will to create and achieve – not to obtain. Desire often has the connotation of an indulgent wish you should be ashamed of. And, if your desires are based around physical objects, selfish gain, or ill-will towards others, perhaps you should be ashamed. There is a big difference between desiring to be the best person you can be in life and desiring to win the lottery. Learn to channel your desire toward good, and use that desire to create something wonderful knowing it came from within you.

Everyone has dreams and goals in life. However, you must also have a sufficient amount of desire around your goals in order to be motivated to achieve them. Many people do not believe their dreams are attainable, and others simply don't want enough out of life to even care. Don't be one of those people! Use your newly developed self-confidence to bolster your courage and get on the path to success!

Now, I recognize we all go through periods in life where our desire, confidence, and motivation take a downward turn. It is at times like these when you need to recognize your innate desire to succeed and harness every bit you can to regain your focus and achieve your goals. Successful people have one thing in common – they desire something and have the motivation to go after it. You have the power to make any dream a reality, if only you can first desire it. Through desire, motivation, and the will to succeed, your dreams will come true, just desire to make them so!

"God did not promise days without pain, laughter without sorrow, or sun without rain, but He did promise strength for the day, comfort for the tears, and light for the way. If God brings you to it; He will bring you through it."

~Unknown

"Faith is not without worry or care, but Faith is fear that has said a prayer."

~Author Unknown

Chapter Five
Faith

"Faith is taking the first step even when you don't see the whole staircase."

~Martin Luther King Jr.

THOUGHTS ON FAITH: Faith is complete and utter belief in something that cannot be scientifically explained or rationalized. It gives you the ability to make a decision or choose a path not based on fact, but from within yourself, influenced by the higher spiritual power you believe in.

My faith in God developed early on in life, and solidified throughout my childhood as I watched my father sink deeper and deeper into the abyss of alcoholism. He was destroying our family and himself at the same time, and I felt there was nothing I could do but rely on my faith and pray. Oftentimes, I would sit in my room late at night, knees folded to my chest praying to God to strengthen our family. I wanted to confront my father about his alcoholism, but I didn't know how to get through to him. Someone once told me that alcoholism is a disease and that abusers must admit their addiction before they can overcome it. I asked God to make my father recognize his illness; I prayed for his health and his healing; and I prayed for the continued strength of my mother, who was bearing the full burden of his illness on a physical, emotional, and financial level.

In this instance, my prayers were not answered. My father continued to abuse alcohol and the strength of our family deteriorated over time. However, it was faith and my belief in God that got me through it. In the darkest of times I still had the comfort of my faith. I will never know the reason why God chose not to intervene and show my father the error of his ways – or maybe he did and my father turned a blind eye – but I believe it happened for a reason. That's the thing about faith, when you blindly believe you also have to blindly accept. As human beings, we don't live our lives in a vacuum. Everything we do or don't do has an effect on someone or something, whether we realize it or not. Take a moment to ponder that statement and recognize its full weight – everything we do or don't do changes someone's life on some level. From the distracted stranger you honked at in traffic, to the hungry child who makes eye contact with you on the street – depending on your actions, you could be the last straw or the last hope for that person. I truly believe if each of us keeps this thought at the forefront of our minds we will be well on our way to changing the world.

I carried my faith to adulthood and when Charlie and I started having children, we made a commitment to instill that same faith in them. I wanted my family to have a belief in God, a sense of the healing prayer can provide in times of trouble, and a trust that God was there to guide them in life. We were always active in the church, because I wanted my children to grow up knowing that God turns no one away and anyone can be a Christian. By embracing the church we had the opportunity to start fresh every day, renew our faith, and ask for forgiveness. We are all sinners, I am living proof of that, but I find comfort in the fact that my faith allows me to seek His guidance and learn from my mistakes. After all, it is through poor judgment and error that we learn the most, and it is through learning and acceptance that we improve our lives.

We become who we are based on our life experiences. I believe a person's faith fluctuates over time and it is tested on a daily basis. However, it is not until our faith is truly tested that we understand the healing and comfort it can provide in times of complete sorrow or despair.

A true test of my faith came in the summer of 1996. It was a busy summer with me teaching swimming lessons for seven hours a day and Charlie spending nearly every daylight hour in the fields. We didn't want the kids to be stuck inside during their summer vacation, so we hired a babysitter to watch them. She was a very responsible young woman and my children absolutely adored her. One beautiful summer evening, while I was in a swim lesson, my son, Austin asked if they could go into town to swim in Lake Eureka. I knew the town provided lifeguards, so I said yes without hesitation. I suggested the babysitter take our Suburban to best accommodate everyone and gave her money to stop for ice cream on the way home. My swim lessons would be finished at 8:00 p.m. and I asked the babysitter to have the children home by that time.

It was 8:00 p.m., 8:15 p.m., and then 8:30 p.m. with no sign of the kids or a call from the babysitter. I knew our babysitter was very responsible, but I couldn't help but worry. Then, almost as if on cue, the phone rang and I felt my consciousness go into slow motion. It was the Eureka Hospital calling to tell me my children had been in an accident, and they had already contacted my neighbor to drive me to the hospital. They wouldn't provide any details over the phone other than my son had been hurt the worst. With the realization that all of my children had to be hurt in order for one of them to be "hurt the worst," my body went numb and I began to shake. That particular evening Charlie was gone and I felt completely alone. Left with only my inner strength and my faith to deal with the situation, I remember falling to my knees and praying to God that everyone would be okay.

Unable to talk, I continued to pray as I traveled the seemingly never-ending road to the hospital. Through my tears, I asked God to be with our children and their babysitter, and to give their bodies strength. As we drove the route to Eureka, we came across a sight that made my heart stop. It was my Suburban, nearly unrecognizable from damage in the ditch. Frozen with fear at the sight of the shattered glass and destroyed vehicle, I had no choice but to expect the worst. The twenty-one mile trip to Eureka seemed like a thousand miles and I was destined to wait an eternity to learn the fate of my children.

As we approached the emergency room, I jumped out of the car and ran inside. I found Austin being attended to, his shirt covered in blood and dirt. I was on the verge of panic when I saw them putting stitches in his head, but Austin looked up at me, smiled and said, "We are all okay, Mom." As a mother, I have never been as thankful for a simple okay as I was in that moment.

Austin had a mild concussion, a broken left clavicle, a two-inch laceration on the top of his head, and a three-inch laceration on his left elbow. Upon assurance from the nurse that he was okay, I looked over to see the babysitter holding

Chapter Six - Perseverance

Elizabeth in a chair. I immediately went over and gave them each a big hug. They each had some minor scrapes and bruises, but thankfully were okay. They were waiting for Alexandra who was downstairs having X-rays. I ran downstairs, opened the door to the X-ray room, and saw her lying on the table. Alexandra looked up at me and said, "Hi, Mom!"

At this moment, when I knew my children would be okay, I fell to my knees and I began to cry, thanking God for watching over our children and their babysitter. After pulling myself together, I walked back upstairs to hear that Charlie was on his way. He had been fishing on the Missouri River that evening and it took them a while to contact him. I eagerly awaited his arrival, wanting his strength and comfort to help me through the situation.

The local sheriff arrived several hours later after the wreck had been cleared and pulled Charlie and me aside. He looked us in the eye and said, "I need to share something with you." He held out his hand and handed me four pennies. I wasn't sure why he was handing me pennies, but he soon explained that he found them at the site of the accident. The sheriff began to cry as he told us the four pennies were lying on the outside running board of the Suburban. All of them had heads facing up and were lying in a straight row. I don't know the significance of it, but my faith does and I have kept those four pennies ever since.

Later, as we talked to the babysitter and the sheriff, we found out what happened – and it scared me to death realizing just how quickly things can happen. As the babysitter was driving, Elizabeth dropped her ice cream cone. The babysitter looked back to see what happened, and as she did, went off the side of the road and over-corrected. The accident report indicated the vehicle flipped three times, ending up on the opposite side of the road facing the wrong way in the ditch. Austin was the only one not wearing his seat belt and was thrown out the back window. Alexandra found him lying at the top of the hill, bleeding badly. She took off her sweatshirt and tied it tightly around his head, applying a technique she had just learned in a first aid class for Girl Scouts. I know we came out lucky that day, and I know God protected my children. This experience made me realize the importance of life above all other things, and it made me realize the faith I put in God is what kept my loved ones safe.

Keys to Implementation

I recognize faith comes from within, and it isn't like other qualities you necessarily learn or teach yourself. However, I do believe you can influence and grow your faith once you have a basic understanding of what you believe. If you want to grow your faith, I suggest three things: strengthen your friendships, be confident in your faith, and continue to focus on the big picture.

Exercise One: Strengthen Your Friendships. Friendships are one of life's greatest gifts. They bring us joy in times of happiness, comfort in times of sorrow, and smiles, hugs, and support during all those times in between. Friendships are also a great tool for deepening your faith in all aspects of life. When you have doubt or question your faith, a friend is your sounding board and confidant. Strengthen your friendships by ridding yourself of all jealousy. Truly appreciate one another's accomplishments and support each other in all that you do.

Focus your energy on making true friends. Acquaintances are plenty and come and go, but true friendship takes time, effort, and nurturing. You will recognize a true friend when, after months of not seeing each other, you bounce right back to where you left off. These friendships are instrumental in your journey to find faith. With the support of true friends in your life, you will come to believe in yourself and always be comforted. Friendships will help you succeed in all aspects of life, including your faith. A true friend is the greatest of all blessings and a gift from God.

"Don't walk in front of me, I may not follow. Don't walk behind me, I may not lead. Walk beside me and be my friend."

~Albert Camus

Exercise Two: Be Confident In Your Faith. My faith is directly linked to my belief in God. Through this belief, I gain confidence and am empowered, strengthened, and energized. Subsequently, it is through this confidence in God I am allowed to achieve anything and everything that He has set out for me. Philippians 4:13 reads: "I can do all things through Him who strengthens me." I have faith that through Jesus Christ I have the power to do anything that is in the will of God. Conversely, if you believe in God, you must also concede that He is under no obligation to enable you to succeed at anything that is not in His will. You must believe in God and put your trust in Him, knowing that if God wants it to happen, it will. Have faith in the path He has set out for you and continually strive toward greatness.

Exercise Three: Focus on the Big Picture. God promises to give you strength and ability. However, if you desire something that is not in God's master plan, you must trust in your faith and move forward. You will be challenged in life; and although you may not see it at the time, use your faith to realize something good comes of all difficult situations. When you focus on the big picture, you allow yourself to learn the important lessons that lie behind the challenges you overcome. God may not reveal the big picture to you all at once, but I truly believe God has a plan for every one of us. Ask Him for guidance and strength.

Through faith, you will find peace in your life. Give Him your confidence and you will realize a higher level of peace and joy in your life. If ever you start to doubt yourself or are fearful of a situation, ask God for strength. It will deepen your faith and make you a stronger person. It is a natural tendency to turn to God only in times of struggle. That is not the answer; you must turn to your faith on a daily basis, not just when you are in trouble. Learn to live through faith on a daily basis and you will be rewarded in life.

Chapter Six
Perseverance

"When the world says, 'Give up,' hope whispers, 'Try' it one more time!"

~Author Unknown

THOUGHTS ON PERSEVERANCE:
This one is simple – NEVER GIVE UP!

As human beings, perseverance is the quality that has allowed us to evolve to the modern age. Without it, our ancestors would have ceased to exist long before our time. Thankfully, when I talk about perseverance in the modern sense, it is in the context of never giving up in the pursuit of a goal and not in the context of actual survival. No goal is achieved without obstacles, and perseverance is the quality that will ultimately allow you to succeed. Every time you are knocked down in life, it is perseverance that makes you get back up, dust yourself off, and start again.

"Being defeated is often a temporary condition. Giving up is what makes it permanent."

~Marilyn vos Savant

"Focus on the solution, not the problem."

~Walter Anderson

I have been tested many times in my life, and I've never questioned my perseverance. I knew I may not always succeed, but it was a given that I would try and try again. One thing I don't understand is how perseverance can almost be innate in some people (like myself), and completely foreign in others. Take my father and me:

As a child, I always knew my father had a drinking problem. Every night our family would sit around the dinner table, and nearly every night his seat was empty. No one ever said anything or asked questions simply because my mom didn't have any answers, and quite frankly, we were used to it. However, the false hope of him joining us for dinner was always present as we sat and ate. My mother always left his dinner plate on the table so when he came home later, drunk, he could sit alone and eat. Despite the excuses my mom would make for him, my instincts as a child told me his behavior wasn't normal. He should want to be home with us and he should want to be a part of our lives. Many nights I sat in my room thinking of things I could do to help him change. After all, I loved my dad...when he wasn't drinking; he was a hard-working, fun man...when he wasn't drinking; and he was cheerful and loving...when he wasn't drinking. Every morning, as I lay awake in bed, I could hear my father downstairs in the kitchen. While I was thankful he made it home safe the night before, the sound of him cracking open the beer he was having for breakfast was like nails on a chalkboard to my ears. My only relief came from the pillow I routinely used to cover my head and drown out the noise.

We tried many times to help my dad by taking him to treatment, but he would never stay. I truly believe my father knew he was an alcoholic, but his love for alcohol was greater than his love for life and therefore he did not want to change. I understand alcoholism is a disease; and as with any disease, there are concessions to be made as a result. However, as the years went on, my father's drinking got worse and he became physically abusive toward my mother. One night, he hit my mother so hard she was knocked unconscious – and that was the last concession our family was willing to make in the name of the disease called alcoholism. It was time to get out.

After my parents divorced, my mother had to work three jobs to raise my two brothers and me, but she never gave up. Learning a lesson from her perseverance, my two older brothers and I all had jobs to help pay for the things we needed for school and to have a little spending money every once in a while. We all worked very hard to make ends meet and that time in our life was hard – but quitting was never an option. We gained confidence and empowerment from knowing that we could persevere in a situation dealt to us by my father, when he didn't even have the perseverance to try to change.

Oftentimes, we didn't know where my father was, and it was the not knowing that continued to make our situation so difficult. We never knew if he was going to show up at our next sporting event, if he was going to call us on the phone, or just show up at our front door. Seeing his abuse of my mother behind closed doors made me realize that when my father was drunk, he could be a very dangerous person. This not knowing was always very frightening to me.

As a high school athlete, I was often in the public eye; and when my father made surprise appearances at my sporting events – drunk and falling up the bleachers – it was very *embarrassing. I knew I had no control over his actions, but I still felt sorry and embarrassed for him. When I was a junior in high school, I ran the 100-meter hurdles at the South Dakota State Track Meet. I was shocked to see my dad there, standing behind the chain link fence. I walked over to greet him right before I was about to run the finals for the 100-meter hurdles, hoping for some words of encouragement and support. He gave a quick hello and then proceeded to tell me that I better win this final race because he had $5,000 bet on me. As I walked away, dumbfounded, I honestly didn't know if he was joking or not; but something deep inside told me he was telling the truth. I won that race, and when I crossed the finish line, I looked up to see his face and he was no longer there. I was heartbroken.*

As I grew older and after Charlie and I married, I didn't have much contact with my father. However, after the birth of our third child, Elizabeth, he asked to come see her. I was surprised but didn't want to deny him the opportunity to see his grandchild. When he arrived, I was shocked at his appearance – he was thin, his skin was discolored, and he was missing teeth. As my dad held Elizabeth I couldn't help but feel that this might be the last time I would ever see him. Our visits were few and far between as it was, and this sudden interest in family was disconcerting. I asked my dad how he was doing and as usual, he said fine. Even if he was not doing well he would always say that he was. I also asked about his drinking, and he still denied having a problem. Tears rolled down my cheeks as my dad left that day. As I stood by the window, waving to my dad, I knew, I just knew that was the last time I would see him. I think deep down he knew it too.

My father passed away two months later from cirrhosis of the liver, a result of his years of alcoholism. I loved my dad, but I will never understand why he gave up on himself and chose to accept his lonely life of alcoholism. He had a loving family who tried everything to help curb his addiction. And, even when we knew it was futile, we still stood by, heartbroken but still supportive.

I believe that good comes from all hardships, and the lessons I learned throughout childhood are why I have a deep desire never to give up. Despite the challenges she faced, my mom never gave up either. She continued to work hard, she believed in and supported us, and most important she taught us the value of never giving up. It is easy to walk away from a difficult situation. It is easy to give up, but my mother never did. She was my inspiration as a child, and she will always be my inspiration as an adult.

We all fail at things in life; however, the only time you really fail is when you give up. If you fail at something, you must pick yourself up and move forward. It takes a positive attitude, determination, confidence, desire, and faith to move on. Keep those five words and their meaning in your head when you feel like giving up. You are a lot stronger than you think, and you will persevere.

> **"When you feel like giving up remember why you hung on so long in the first place."**

~Unknown

In addition to your own perseverance in life, it is also very important to encourage others not to quit when they are on the brink of failure. Your support can be the difference between success and failure. We raised our children not to be quitters and to always persevere. However, that doesn't

Austin Hoffman, graduate of South Dakota State University
Photo by Jolosch Photography

mean we aren't all tested. Our oldest child, Austin, had just finished his second year of college and told us he wanted to quit. He didn't know what he wanted to do in life and honestly, felt it was a waste of time and money to continue. I remember our conversation well, and I told him very specifically that he was not going to quit. I didn't care if I had to pay for his rent for another ten years, but he was staying in school. (Of course, my first mistake was offering to continue to pay his rent because he made sure of that!) More important, he stayed in school. Sure, he changed his major several times; but the important thing was that he kept going and kept trying to find his place in life. After his college graduation ceremony, he came up to me, gave me a hug, and said, "Thank you, Mom, for not letting me quit." He is now a very successful man who utilizes perseverance in his everyday life.

Life is a test. A tough one sometimes, but you must persevere. You may experience self-doubt and feel lost at times, but use your faith to realize better times may be right around the corner, and you can't get around that corner if you quit. Never stop believing and remind yourself of your amazing potential. Few good things in life come easy, and nearly everything worth attaining requires hard work and perseverance. Often the only obstacle between you and something better is simply not giving up. No matter how impossible your goal may be, no matter how unattainable others may think it is, and no matter how many times you have been rejected, take the first step forward and never give up on your dreams.

Austin and Megan Hoffman
Photo by Shalista Photography

"Never consider the possibility of failure; as long as you persist, you will be successful."

~Brian Tracy

We all will consider giving up at some point in our lives; these thoughts are inescapable. At times when we don't meet our own expectations and feel discouraged, we will surely hit a wall of self-doubt. It is at that point you must take the easy option out of the equation – the option of giving up. Once you've quit the first time, it is way too easy to quit a second time. Life is comprised of struggles and hardships, but it is how we react and persevere that creates the quality of our life. Believe in yourself to NEVER GIVE UP!

Conclusion

There have been times in my life when I hit points lower than I ever thought possible. I felt completely alone and seriously contemplated whether or not I could go on. I actually considering quitting – something I don't do. At those low points in my life I found my greatest strength came from the support of others and the encouragement they extended to me. For example, I was in a stressful situation a couple years ago and felt as though quitting was my only option. As a last effort to emerge from the situation with the dignity of not being a quitter, I consulted a friend and mentor guidance. After I explained my situation and all the reasons why I had no choice but to quit, he looked me straight in the eye and said, "Holly, you do not look like a quitter to me."

It was those words spoken out loud that triggered my memory. I was instantly transported back in time to my sixth grade year when my parents were going through a tumultuous divorce. I was young; I wanted my family to be like everyone else's. I wanted to perform at school functions and see my parents sitting there together in the front row, clapping for my accomplishments and being proud. Alas, my family was not like everyone else's, and I had to be content with a father who came home drunk while my mom was working at one of her three jobs. At that young age, I came to the stark realization that there are things in life I can't control, and in light of this particular situation that my life would never be the same. Even though I didn't like it, my parents' divorce was inevitable and something I had to accept. I also realized I was a lot stronger than I thought, and it was during this time I adopted the mindset to never give up, no matter the fight. I had to live with my parents' divorce, and while the disappointment was immense, I understood the healing process could finally begin.

It is kind of funny the way life circles you back to the hard life lessons when you begin to unlearn them. At times in life when I was truly tested, it was the remembrance of my sixth grade year that made me realize I could not quit. I wasn't a quitter back in sixth grade and I'm certainly not a quitter now. I used those memories to call upon every last cell of my inner strength to keep from quitting, and time and again, I continue to be surprised at how strong I really am.

I have reached a point in my life where I can look back and say that I have achieved some great things. I have experienced being a daughter, sister, wife, parent, coach, and mentor; I have conquered challenges and been on adventures; and I have lived a spiritual life. Truth is, none of us know when our last day will come, which is why I choose to live every day to the fullest and not to dwell on the past. I make an effort to infuse positive thoughts into every day, and it is amazing how my attitude, confidence, determination, desire, and ultimately my life has changed.

Success doesn't come easy. It takes a positive attitude, determination, confidence, desire, faith, and perseverance to achieve your goals. We all fail at things in life; however, the

Conclusion

only time you really fail is when you give up. My advice is simple: never give up. By living each and every day to the fullest you will realize the cycle of success and all the amazing ways it can change your life. I hope this book encourages you to believe in yourself. I want you to carry this book with you every day, so if you are feeling discouraged, you can read your favorite passage or quote and feel inspired to embrace the challenges and opportunities in your life. By doing so you will:

- Develop a positive attitude and manage negative influences in your life

- Harness your determination to achieve and maintain success

- Focus on your strengths and develop a high level of self-confidence

- Identify your true desires in life which build the foundation of your goals

- Build a strong family of faith, love, and harmony

- Shed false limitations and persevere

I hope by reading this book you will learn to own your inner strength and embrace your winner within.

You are special . . .

You are a winner . . .

You can be the person you've always wanted to be!

About the Author

Holly (Wanner) Hoffman was born and raised in Eureka, South Dakota, a small town with about 850 residents in  north central South Dakota. In the eighth grade, Holly discovered a passion for running and repeatedly earned statewide recognition for her athletic abilities, including Female High School Athlete of the Year in 1984. After attending Northern State University in Aberdeen, South Dakota, Holly married Charlie Hoffman and the couple established their first home on a cattle ranch in rural McPherson County. Son Austin and daughters Alexandra and Elizabeth soon completed the Hoffman family. In 1994 Holly started a swim team in the Eureka community, which quickly became a well-known swim team across the state. Holly coached the swim team for 17 years (volunteering her time for 16 of the 17 years). She was named Coach of The Year twice.

Austin fishing in Alaska

Charlie and Austin fishing in Alaska

Elizabeth swimming for the
University of South Dakota

Alexandra swimming for
South Dakota State University

Austin Hoffman, Megan Hoffman, Elizabeth Hoffman, Alexandra Hoffman and John Bisson front row: Holly Hoffman and Charlie Hoffman

Alexandra Hoffman
2006 Miss South
Dakota Teen USA
Photo by Solberg
Photography

Elizabeth Hoffman
2008 Miss South
Dakota Teen USA
Photo by Solberg
Photography

Holly Speaking
Photo by Photography
by Jocelyn

Charlie & Holly in St. Lucia

MOTIVATIONAL & INSPIRATIONAL SPEAKER

ATTITUDE
DETERMINATION
CONFIDENCE
DESIRE
FAITH

You did a fantastic presentation at ASHH Heart Days! Your adventure and sharing about reaching deep down in yourself was so inspiring. Employees continue to rave about your talk. You made a difference in me – in how I view the world – more opportunities and engaging – and most importantly the value of family and priorities in life. Thanks again! ~Jean Hunhoff, Yankton SD

My wife and I thoroughly enjoyed your presentation Tuesday night in Arlington, SD. You help us to remember what is important. We get so wrapped up in the hustle and bustle of our daily lives that we sometimes don't appreciate all we have the way we should. Once again, thank you for an excellent presentation. ~LaMonte McCuen, Castlewood, SD

For more information on booking Holly Hoffman for your next event, please visit www.hollyhoffman.org